FOLLOW US ON
INSTAGRAM
@KindergartenEducation

THIS NOTEBOOK BELONGS TO:

MORE BOOKS BY SMART KIDS NOTEBOOKS
(SCAN THE QR CODE OR VISIT: bit.ly/smartkidsnotebooks)

TRACE THE LINE
TO CONNECT BOTH SIDES

TRACE THE LINE
TO CONNECT BOTH SIDES

TRACE THE SHAPES

TRACE THE SHAPES

CONNECT THE DOTS
AND COLOR THE IMAGE

CONNECT THE DOTS
AND COLOR THE IMAGE

CONNECT THE DOTS
AND COLOR THE IMAGE

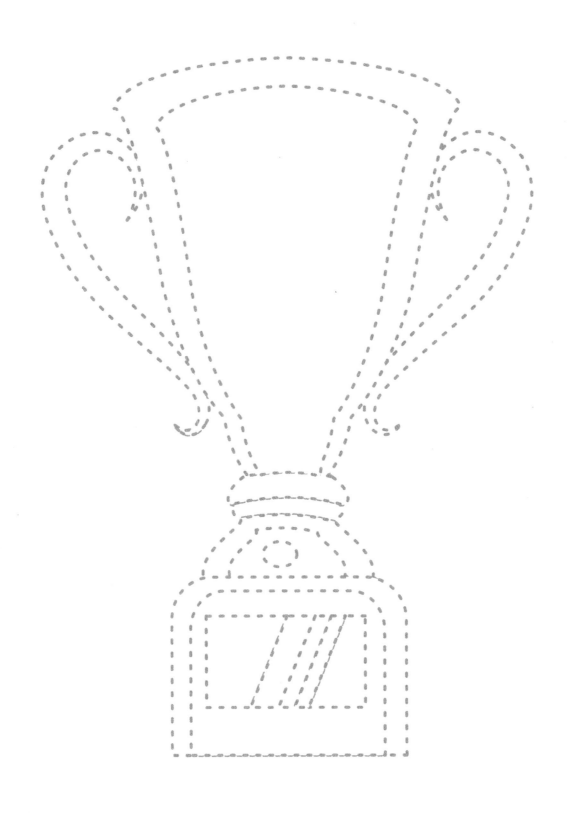

CONNECT THE DOTS
AND COLOR THE IMAGE

CONNECT THE DOTS
AND COLOR THE IMAGE

CONNECT THE DOTS
AND COLOR THE IMAGE

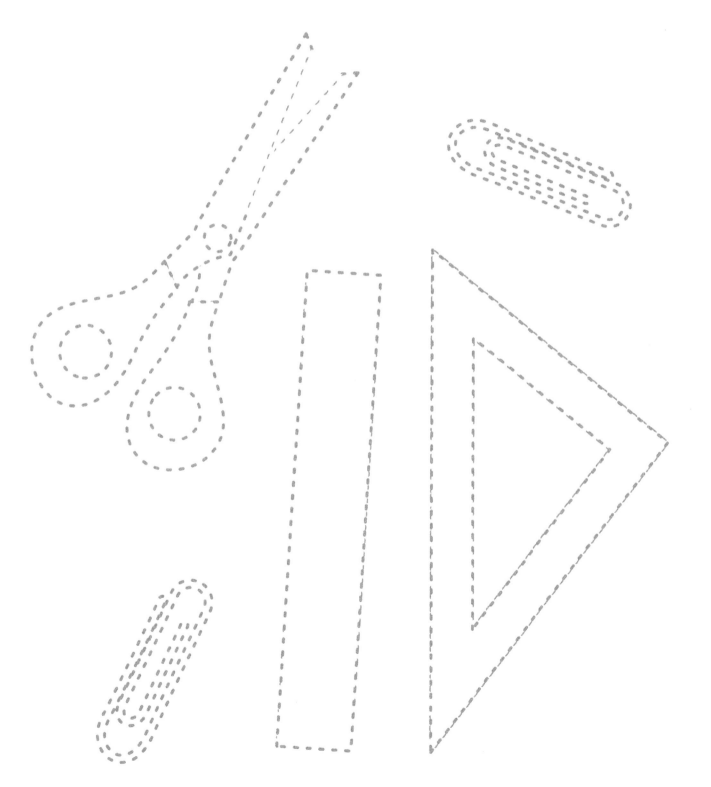

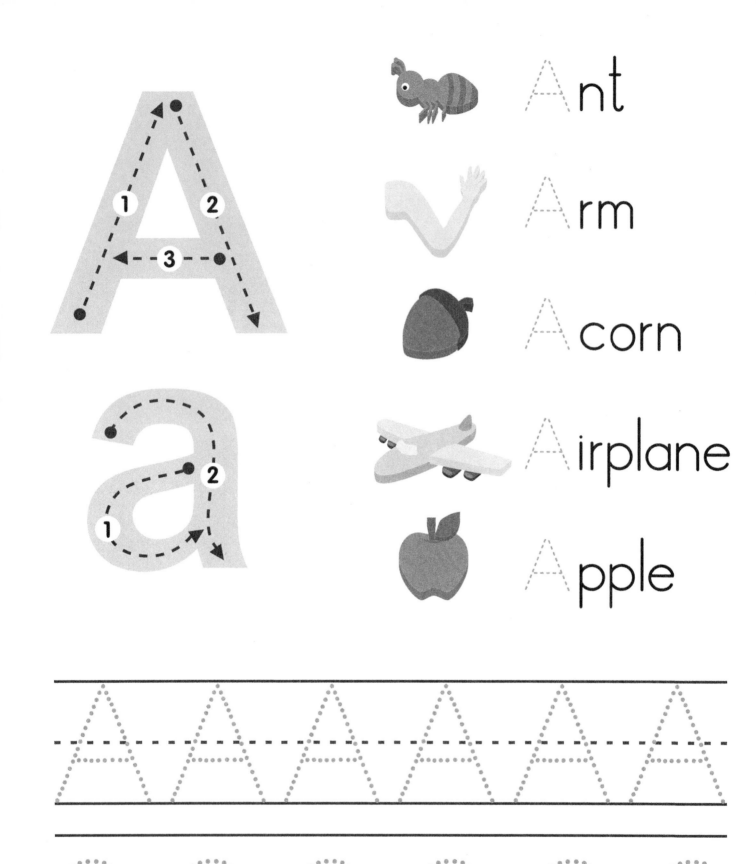

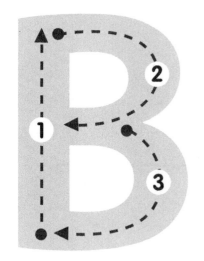
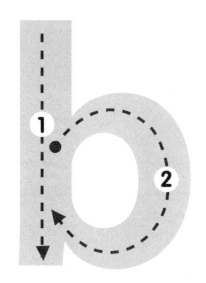

 Book

 Bee

 Ball

 Butterfly

 Backhoe

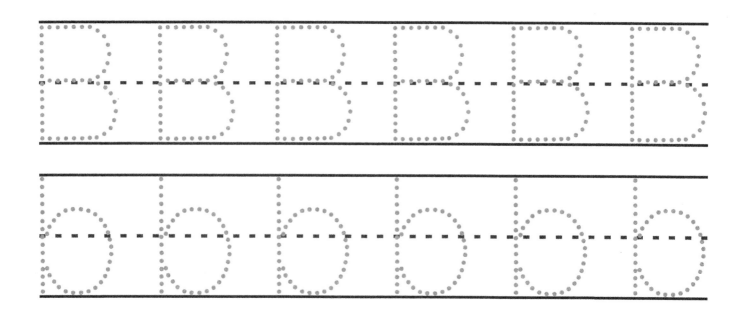

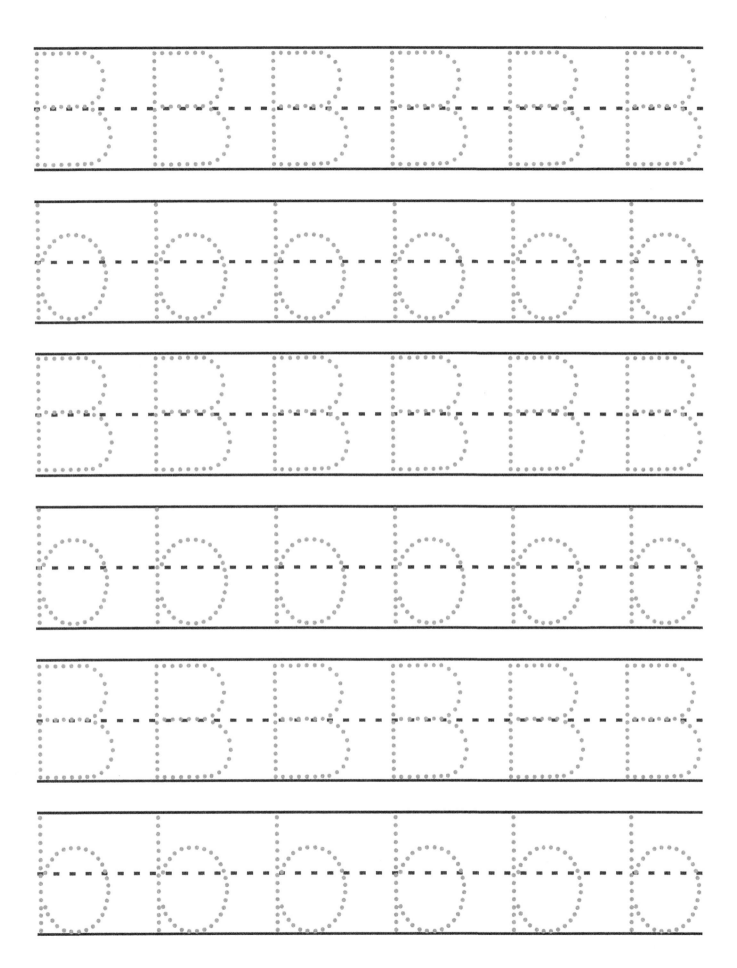

# Car
Cake
Carrot
Clock
Cloud

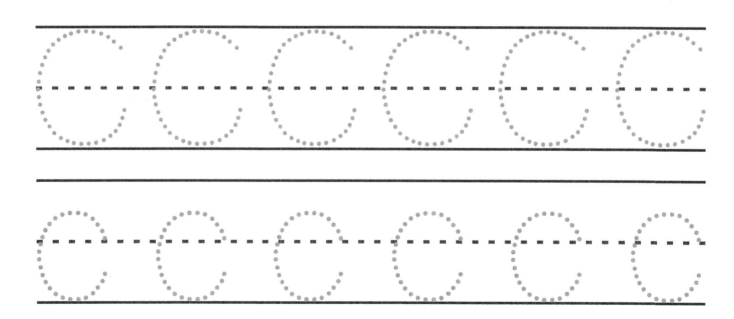

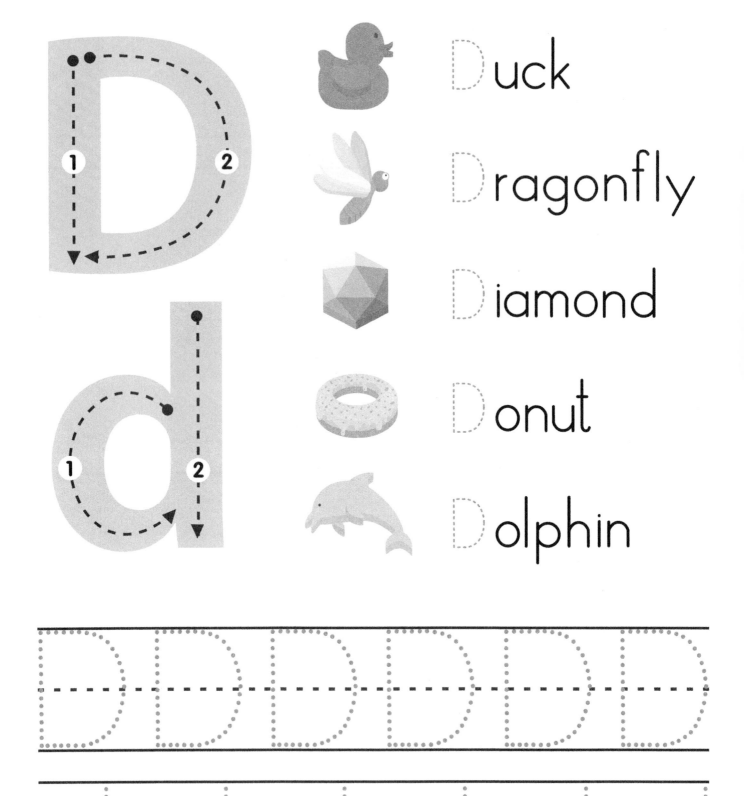

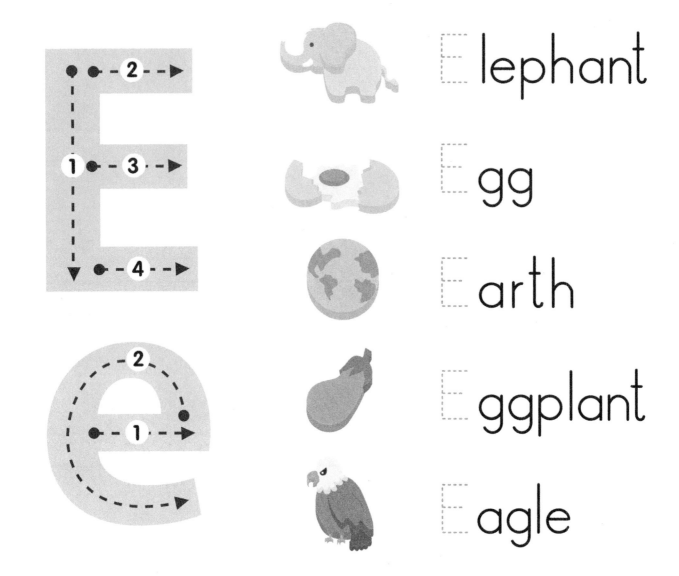

Elephant

Egg

Earth

Eggplant

Eagle

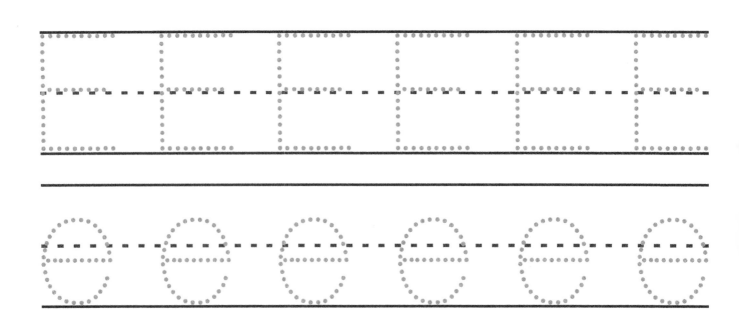

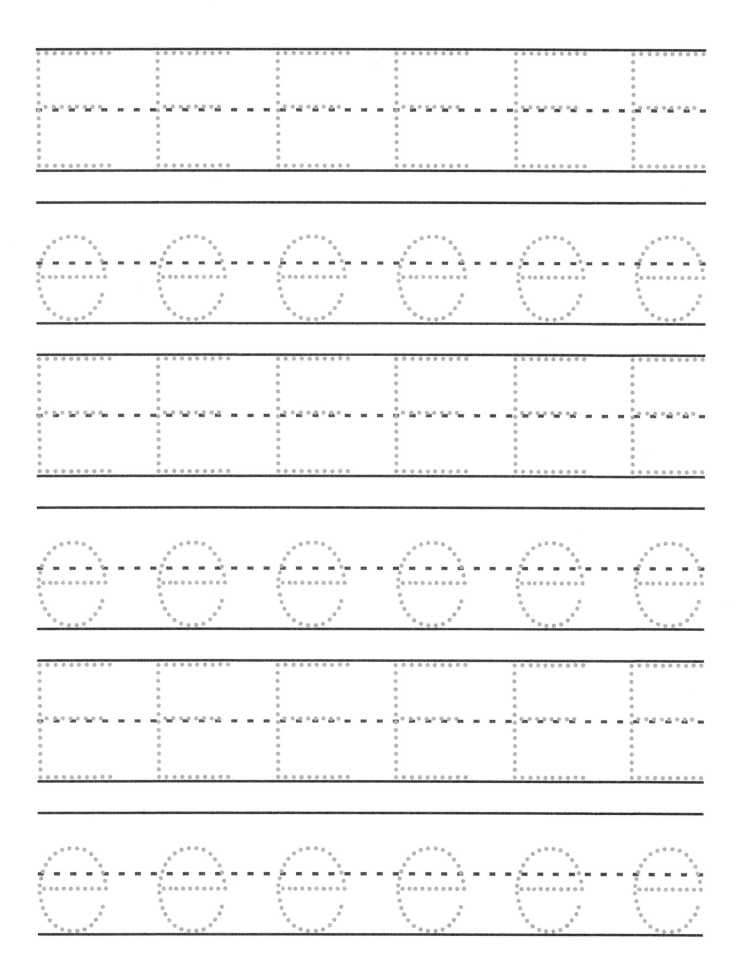

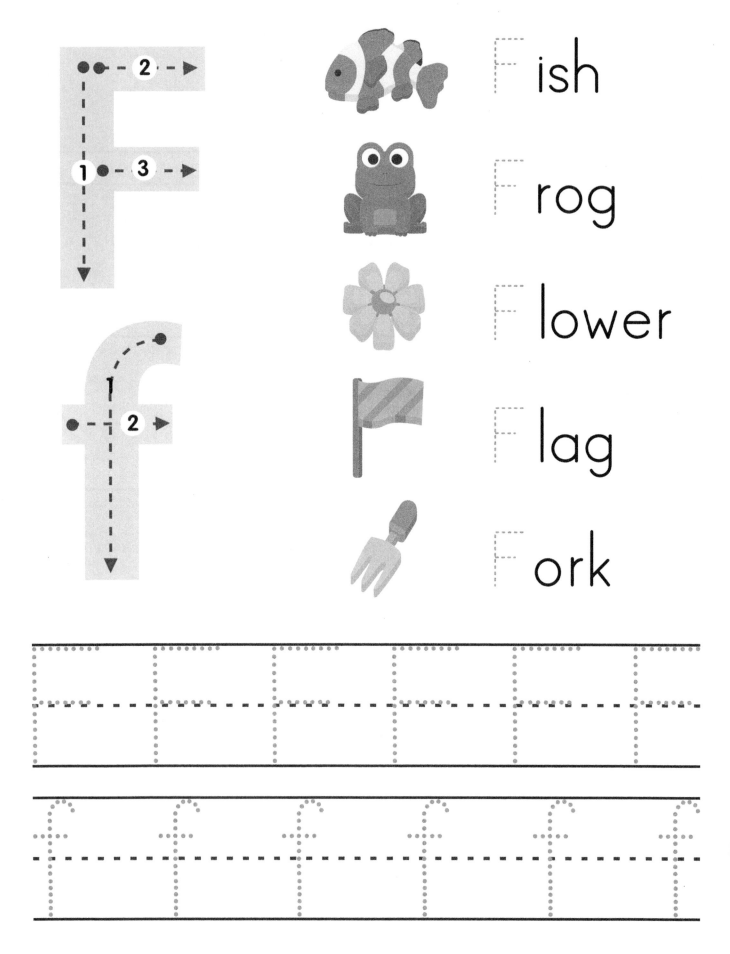

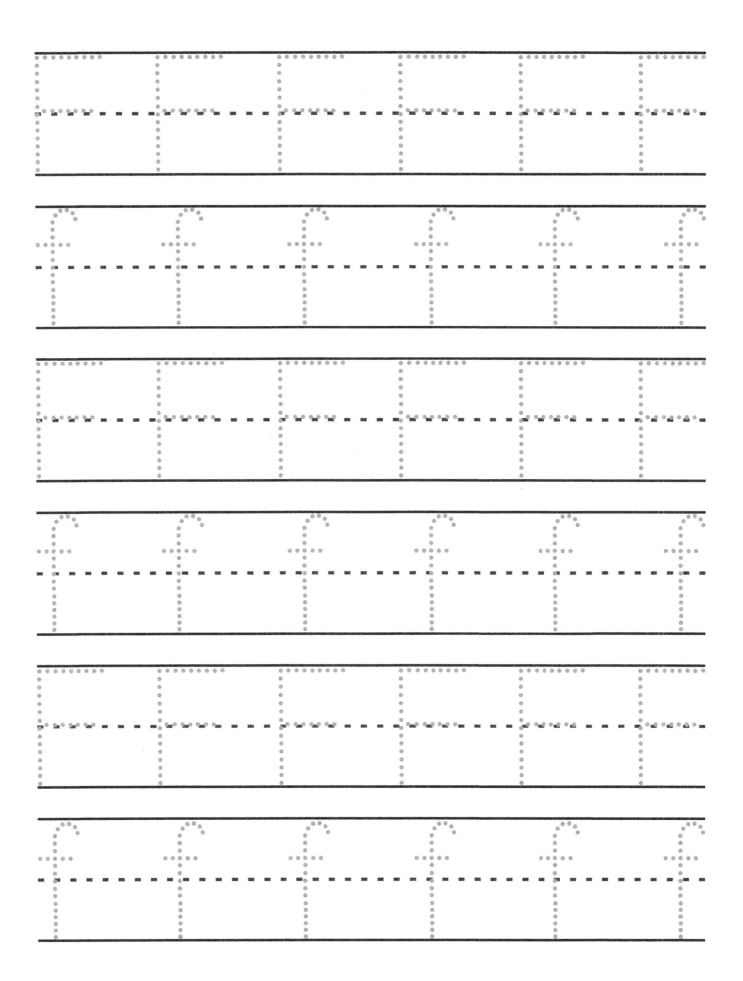

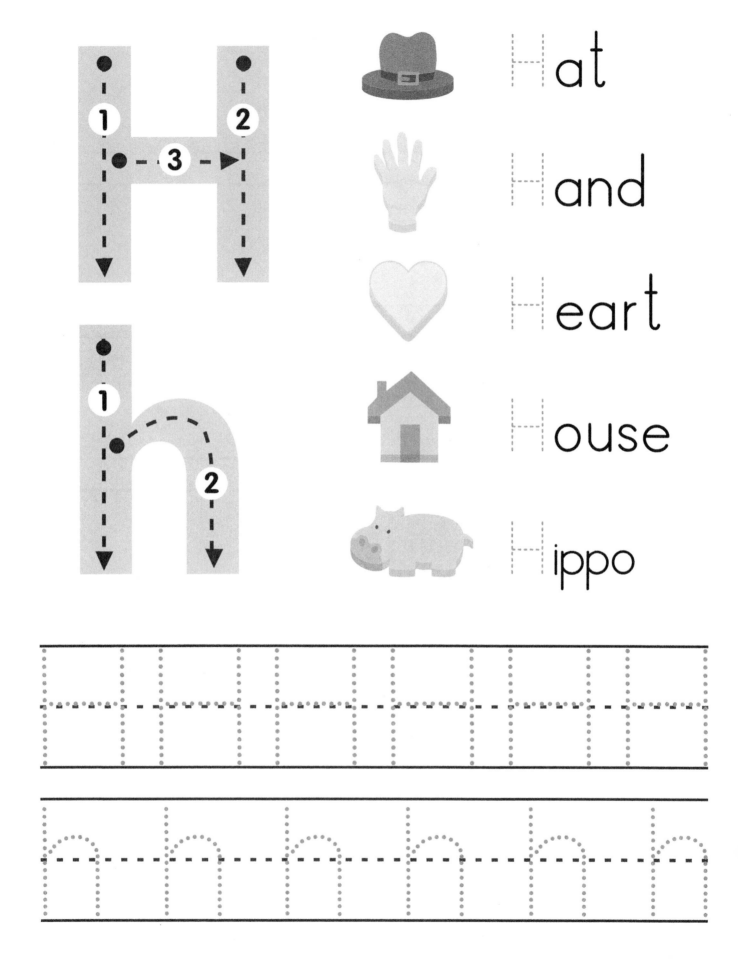

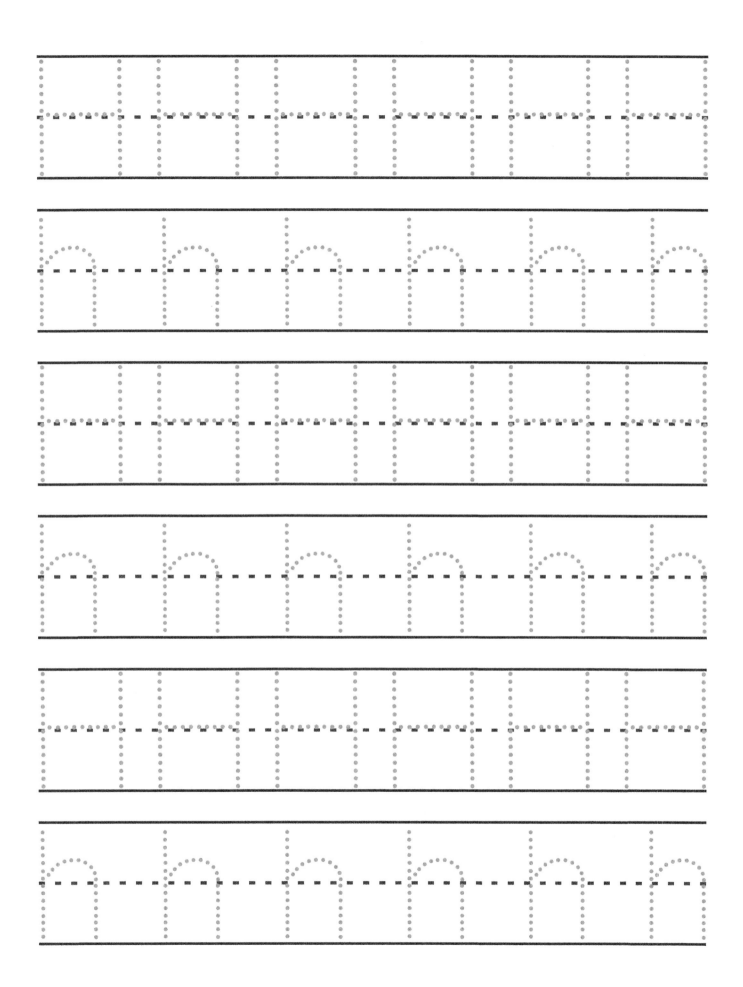

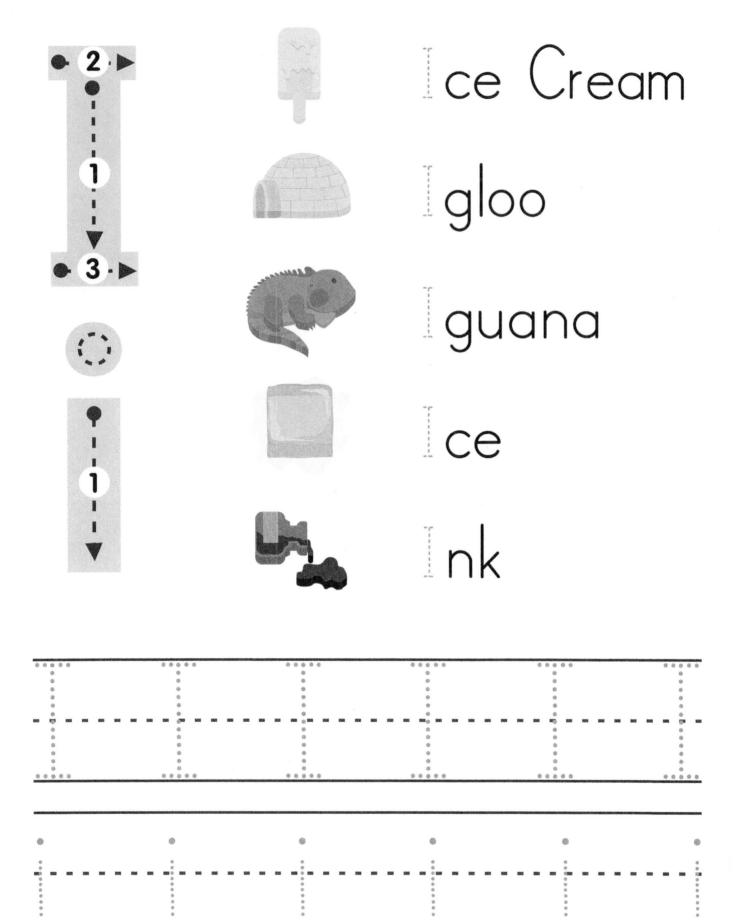

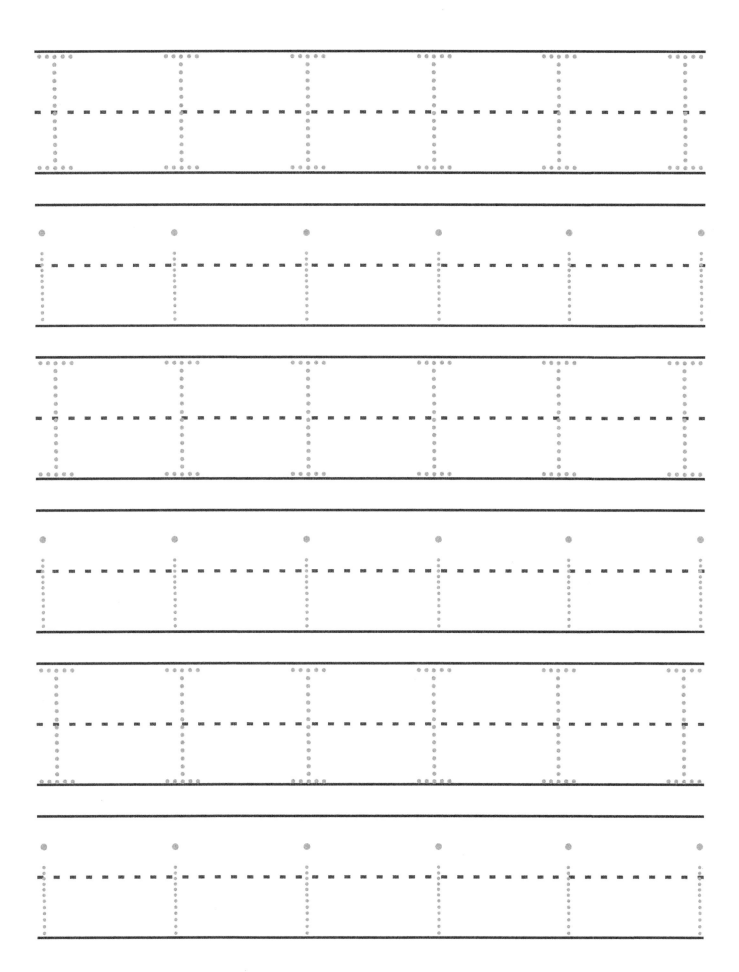

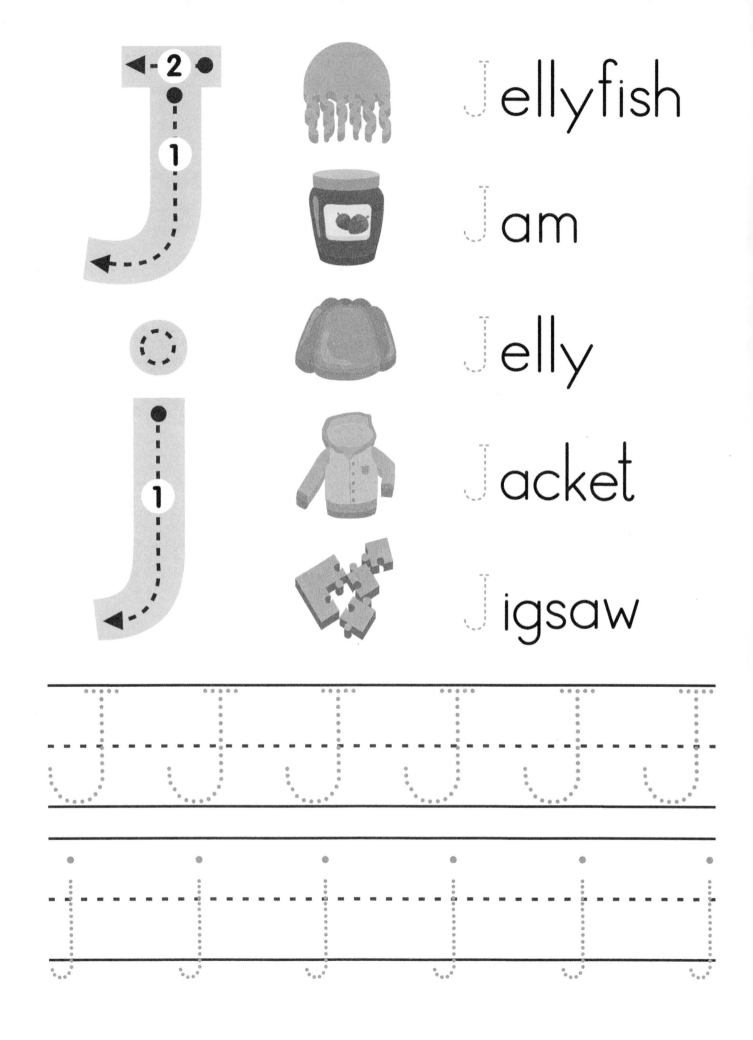

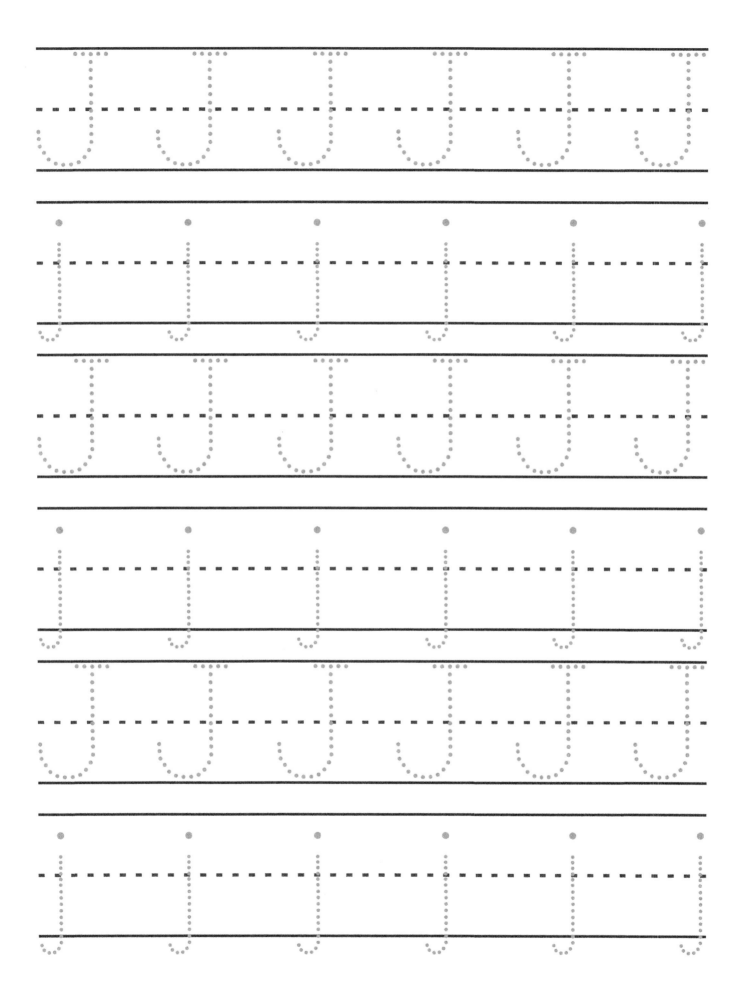

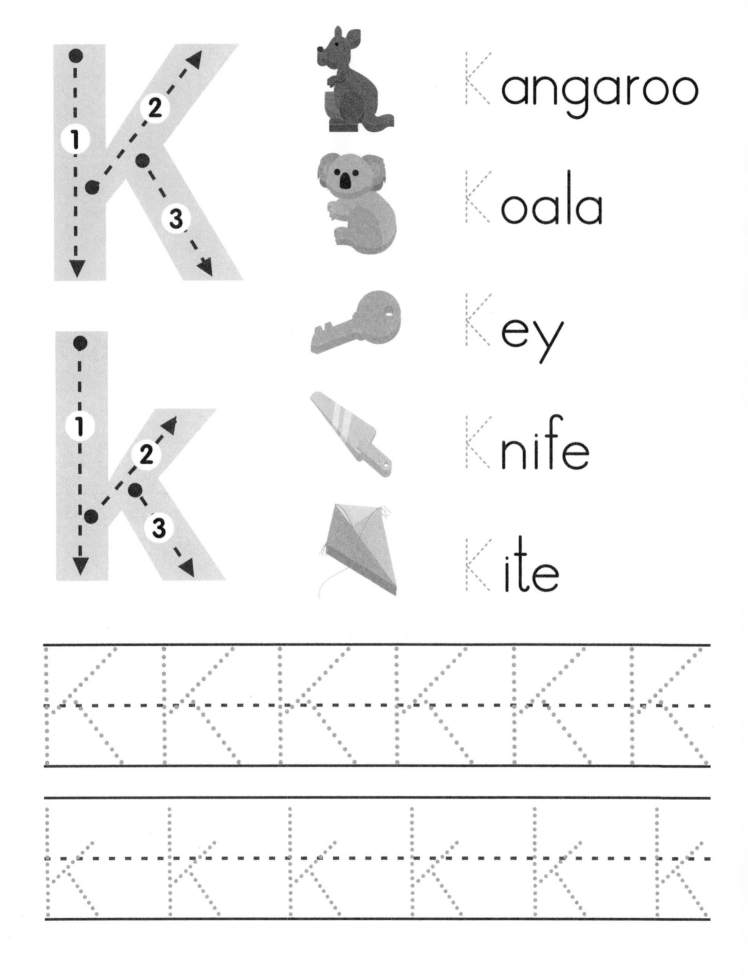

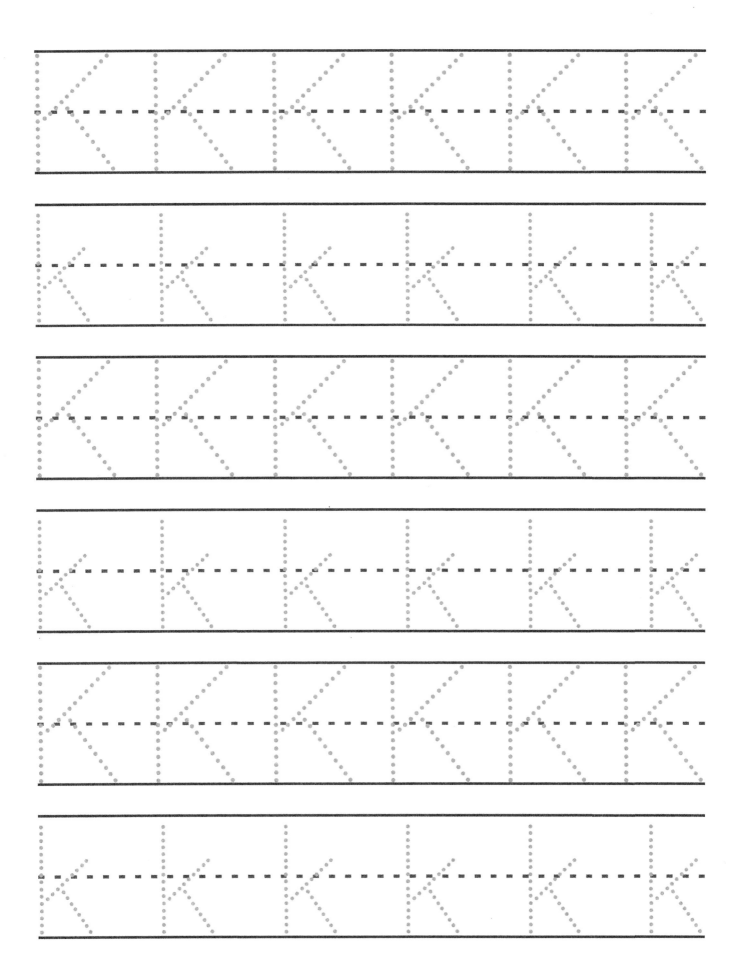

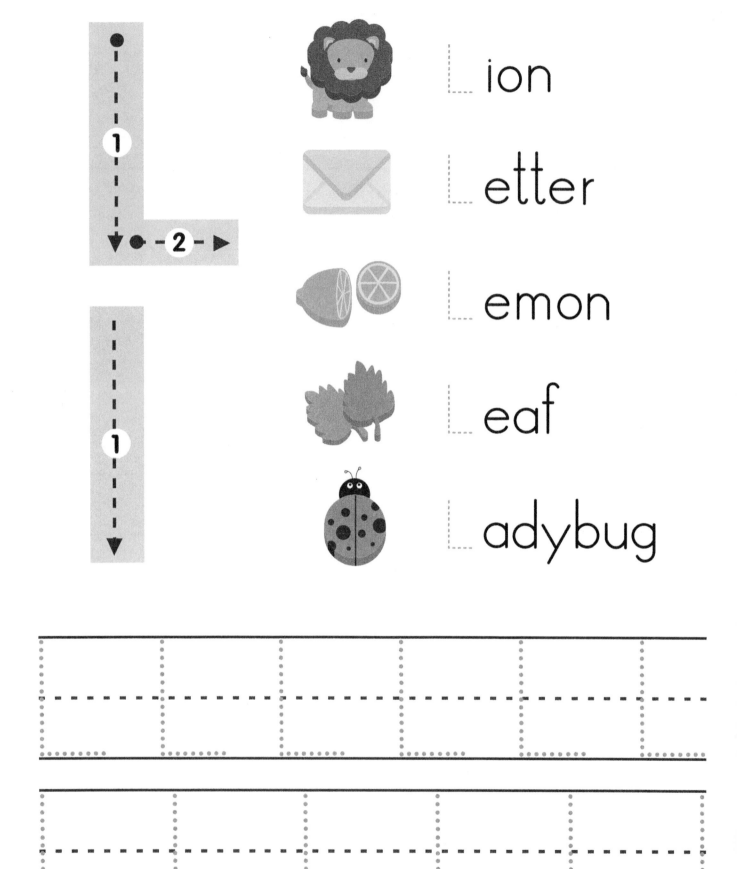

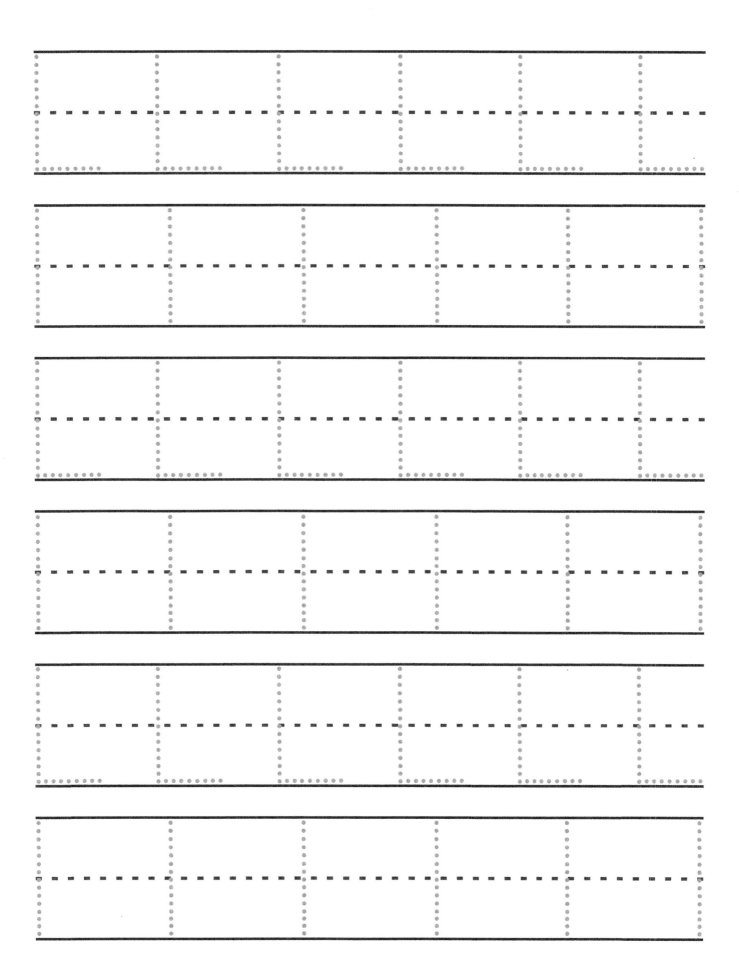

MMMMMMM

mmmmmmm

MMMMMMM

mmmmmmm

MMMMMMM

mmmmmmm

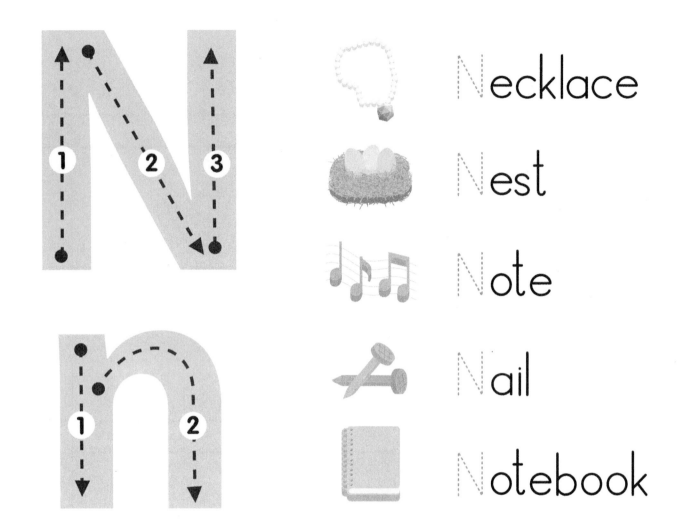
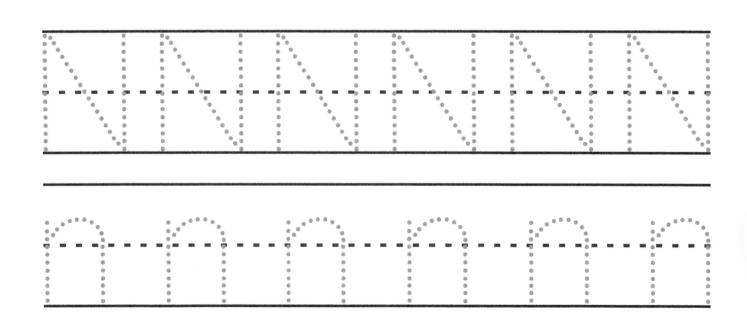

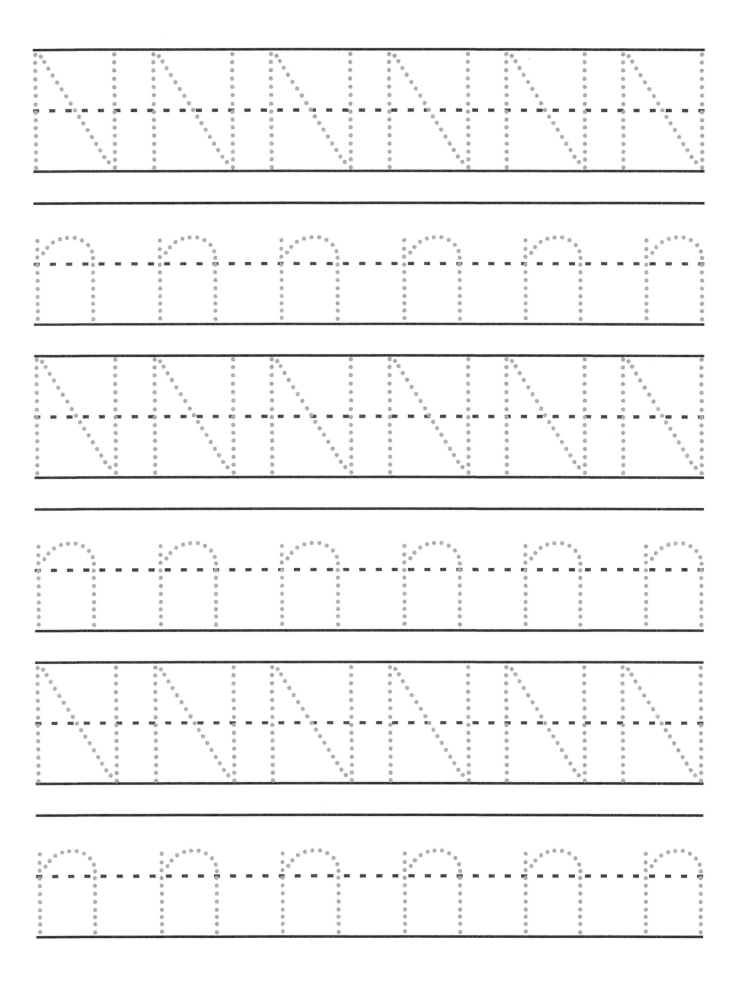

Owl
Octopus
Orange
Ostrich
Orchid

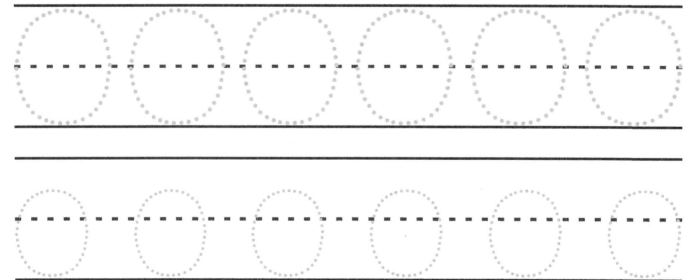

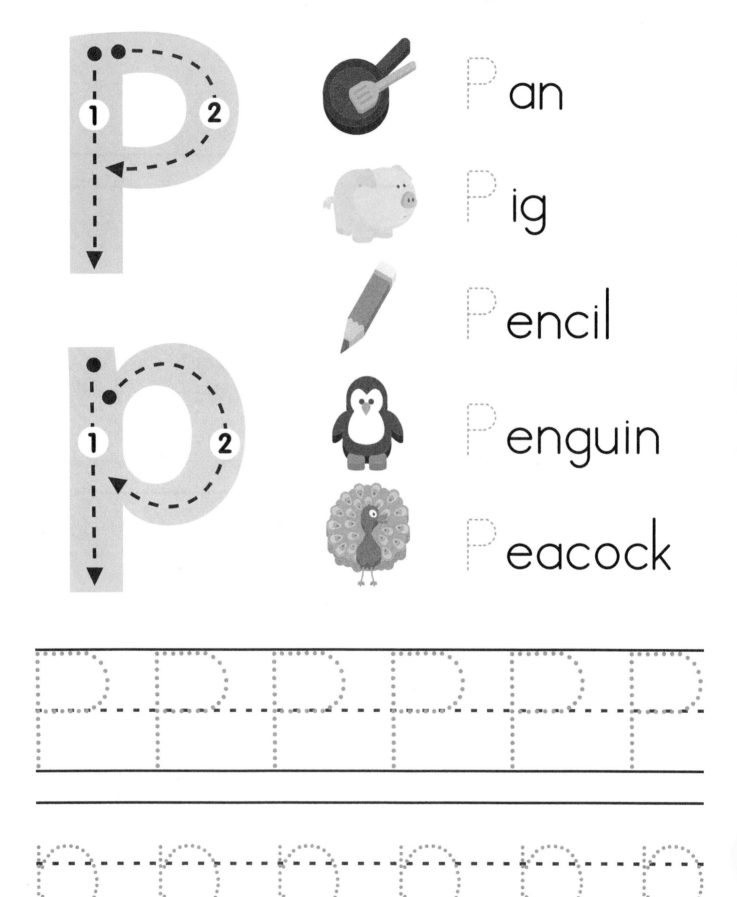

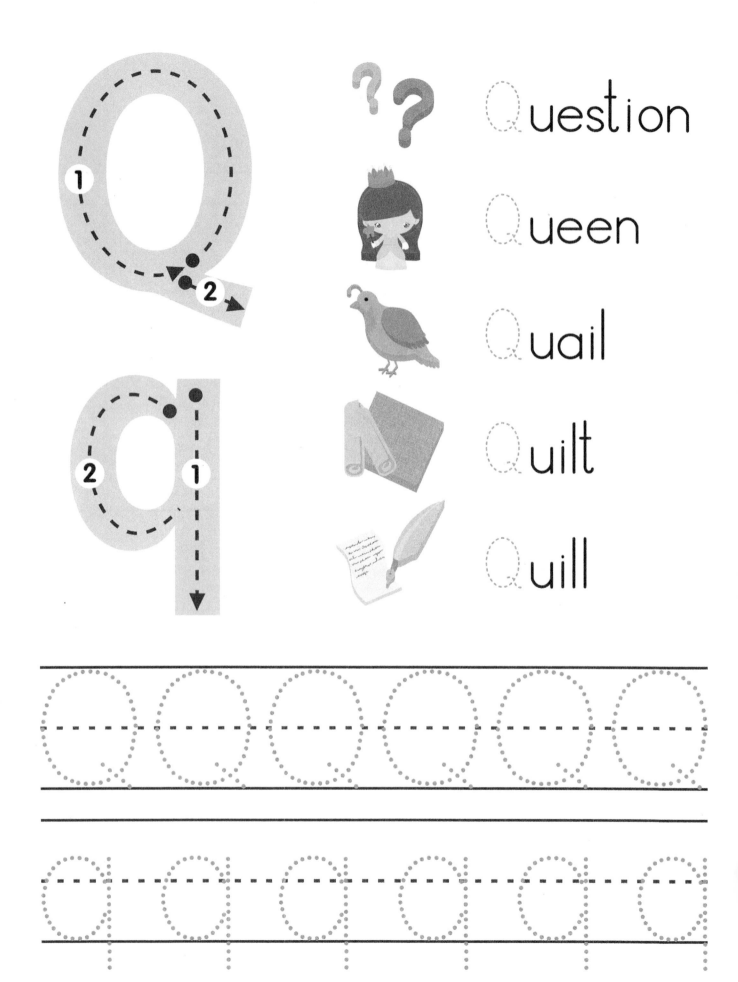

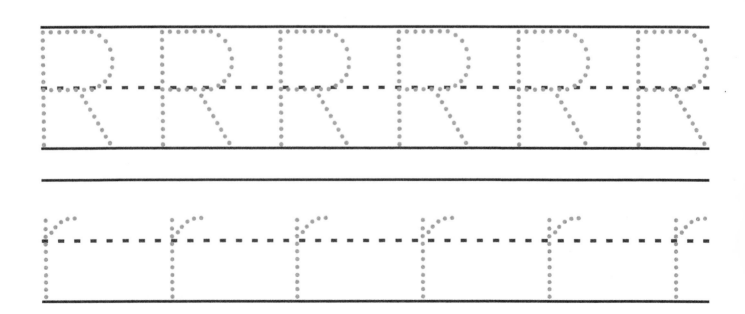

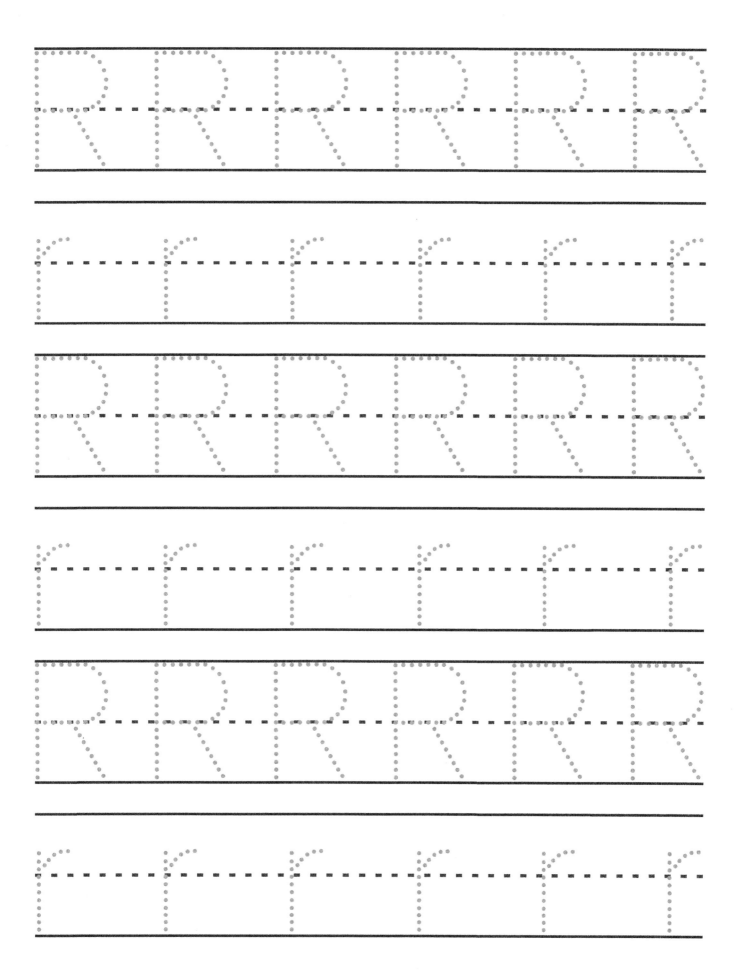

Strawberry
shirt
slide
snail
sun

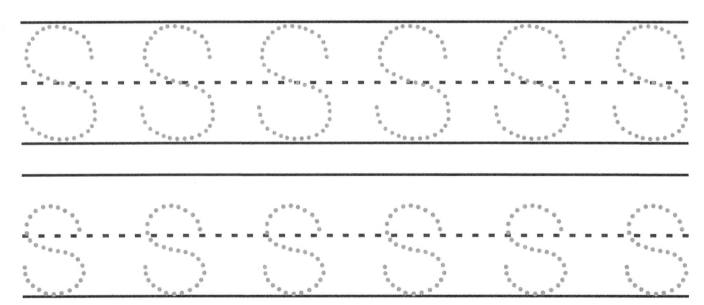

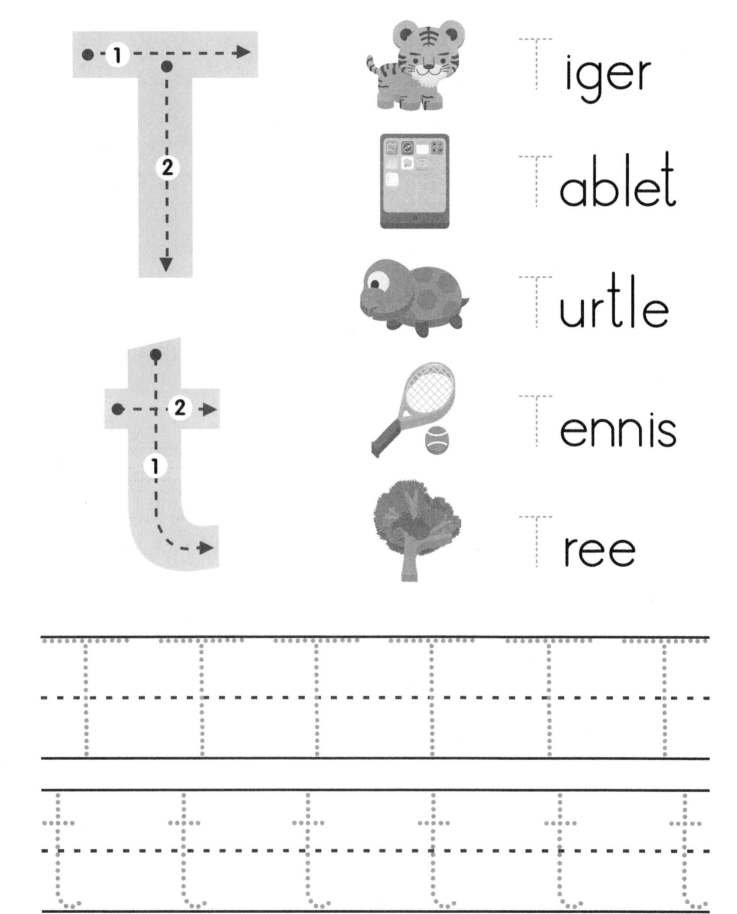

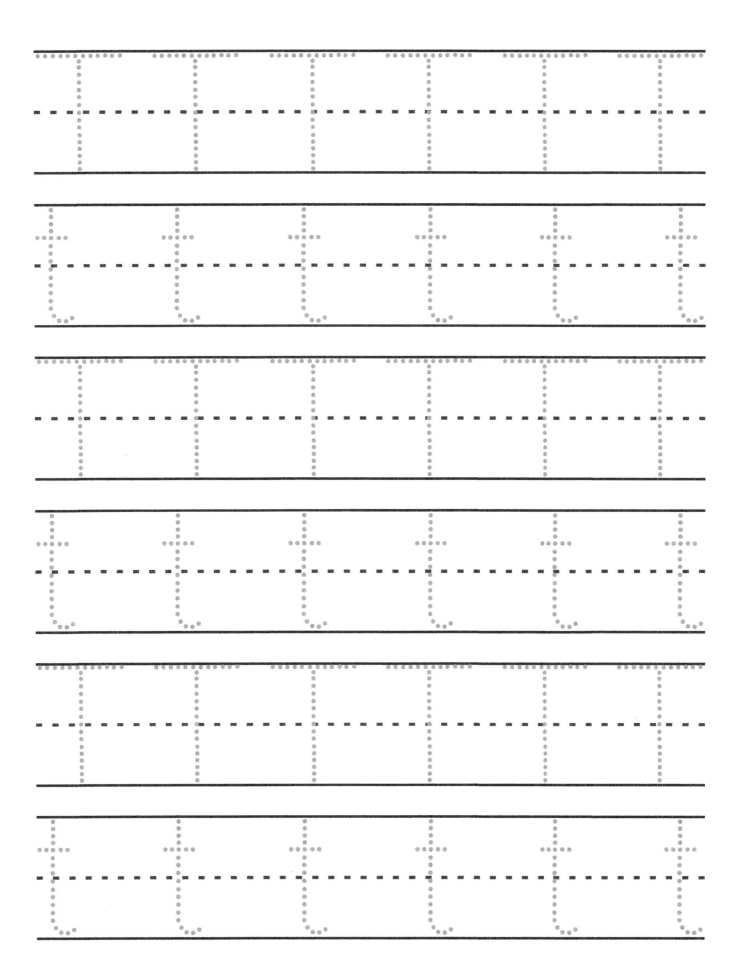

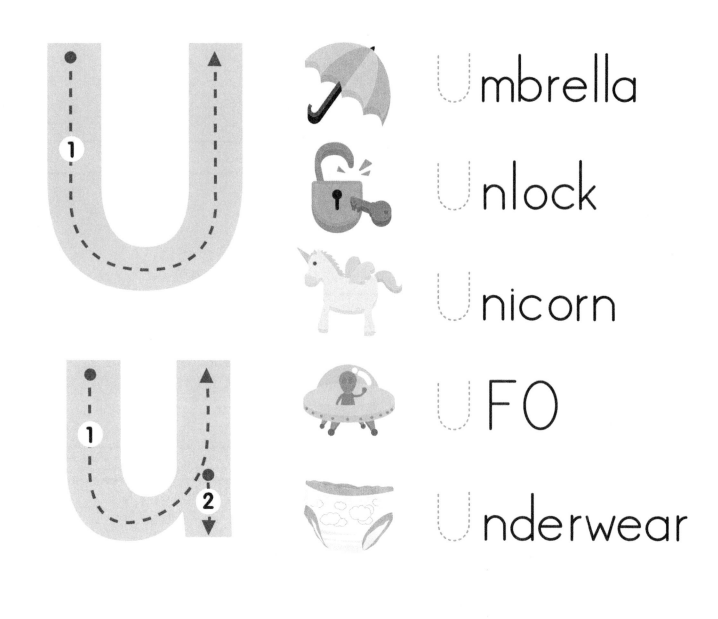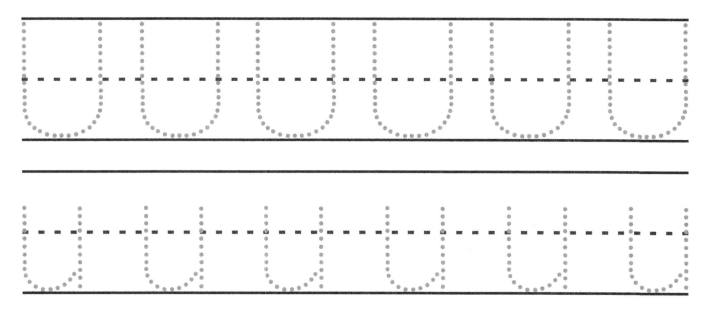

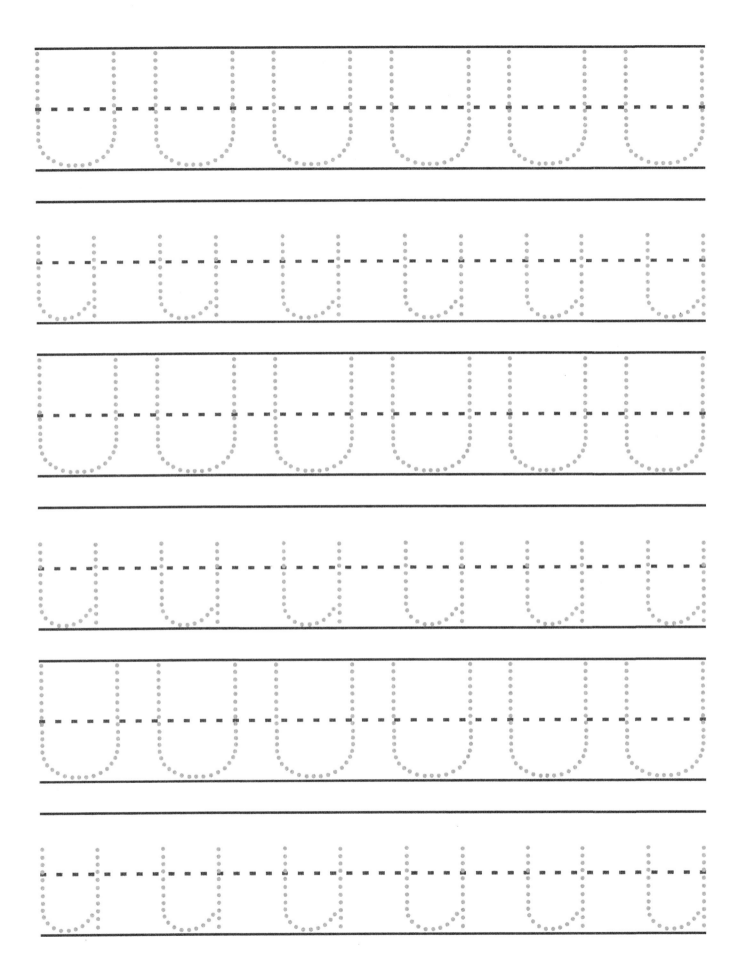

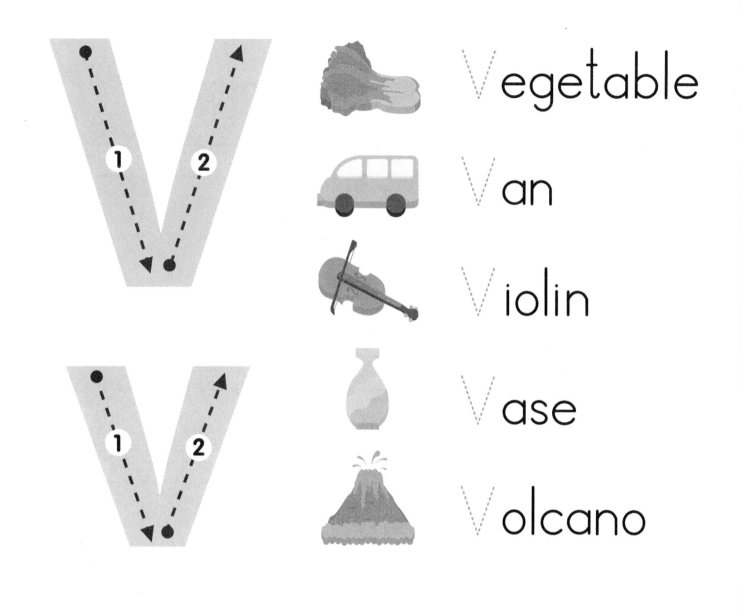

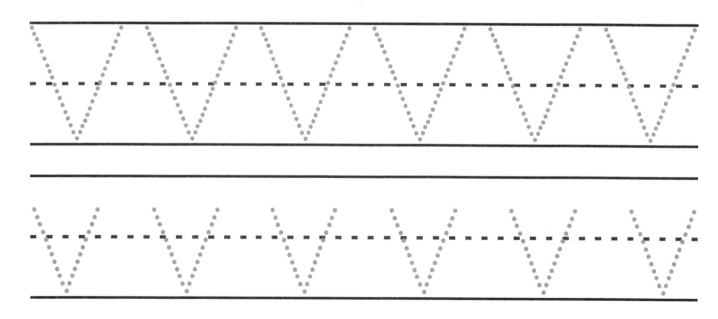

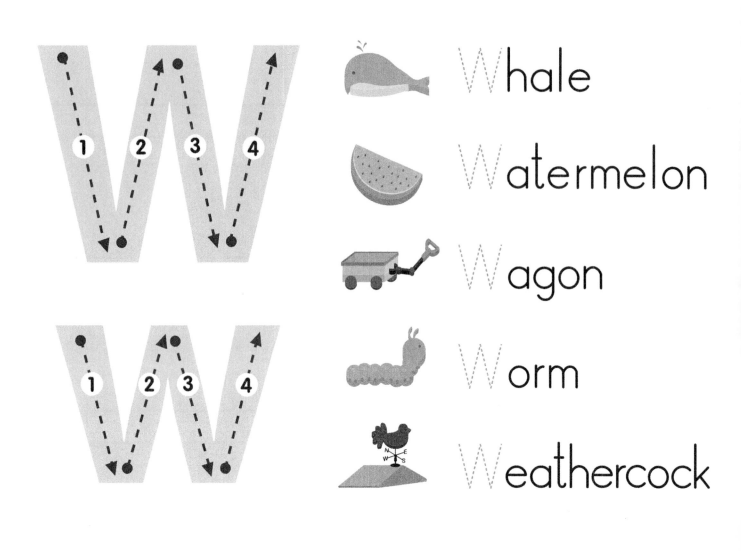

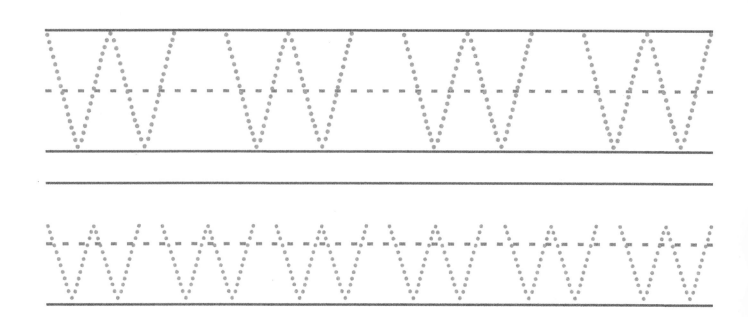

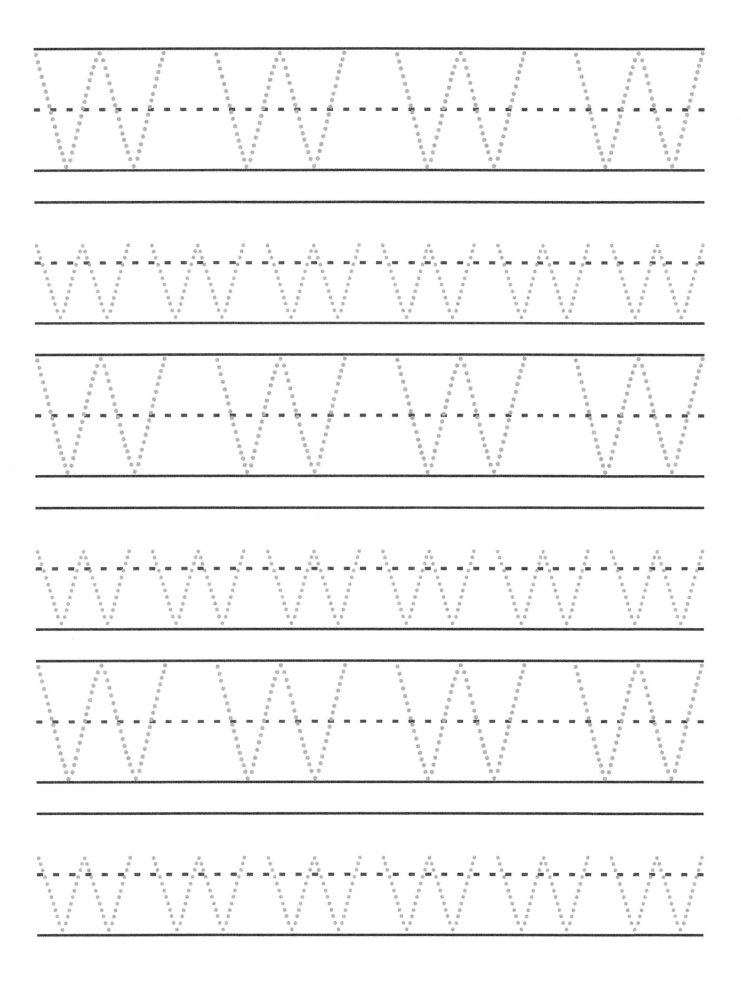

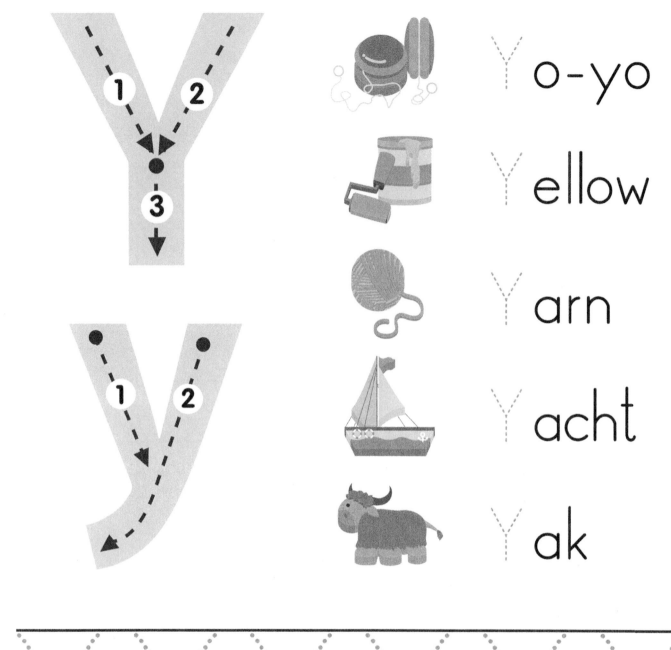

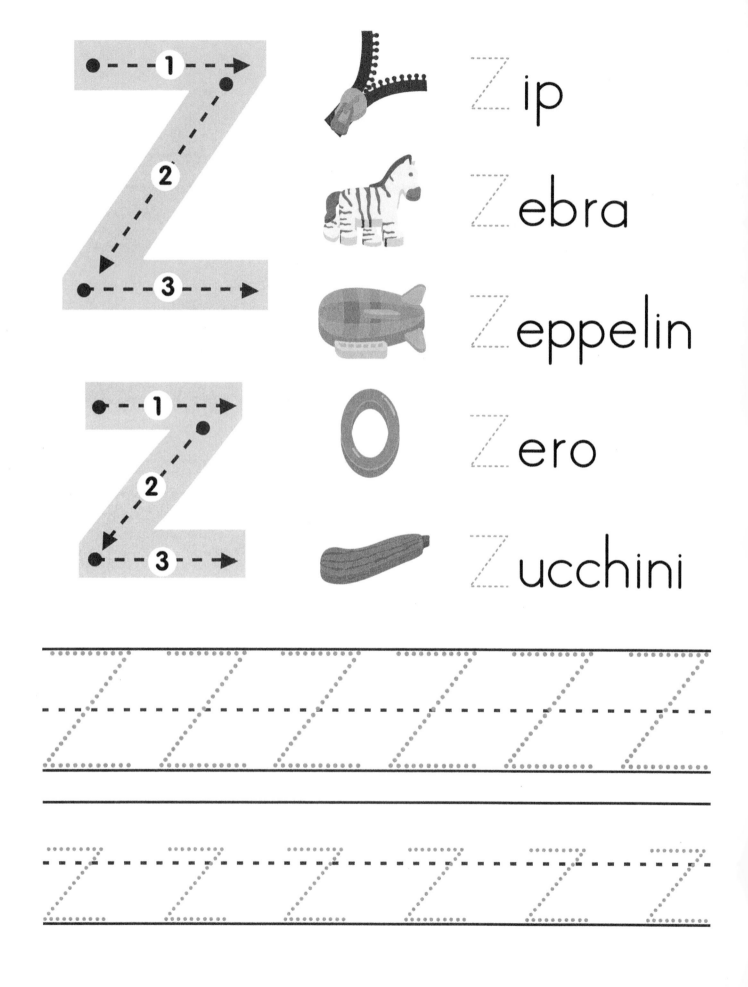

PRACTICE ON YOUR OWN

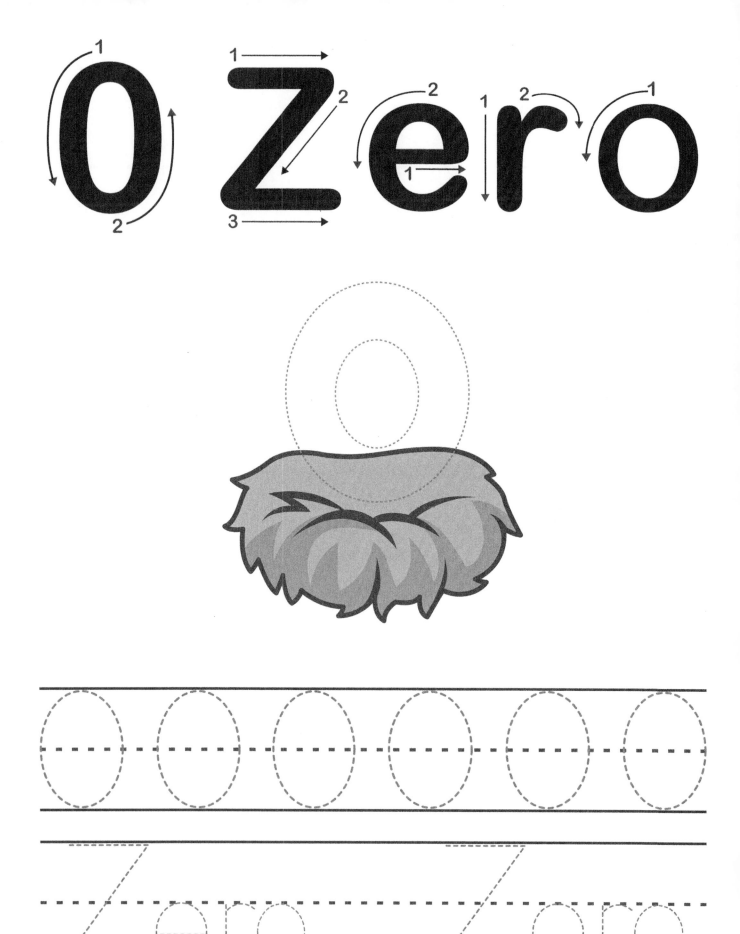

1 1 1 1 1 1

One One One

1 1 1 1 1 1

One One One

1 1 1 1 1 1

One One One

2 2 2 2 2

Two Two Two

2 2 2 2 2

Two Two Two

2 2 2 2 2

Two Two Two

3 Three

3 3 3 3 3 3

Three Three

4 Four

4 4 4 4 4 4 4

Four Four Four

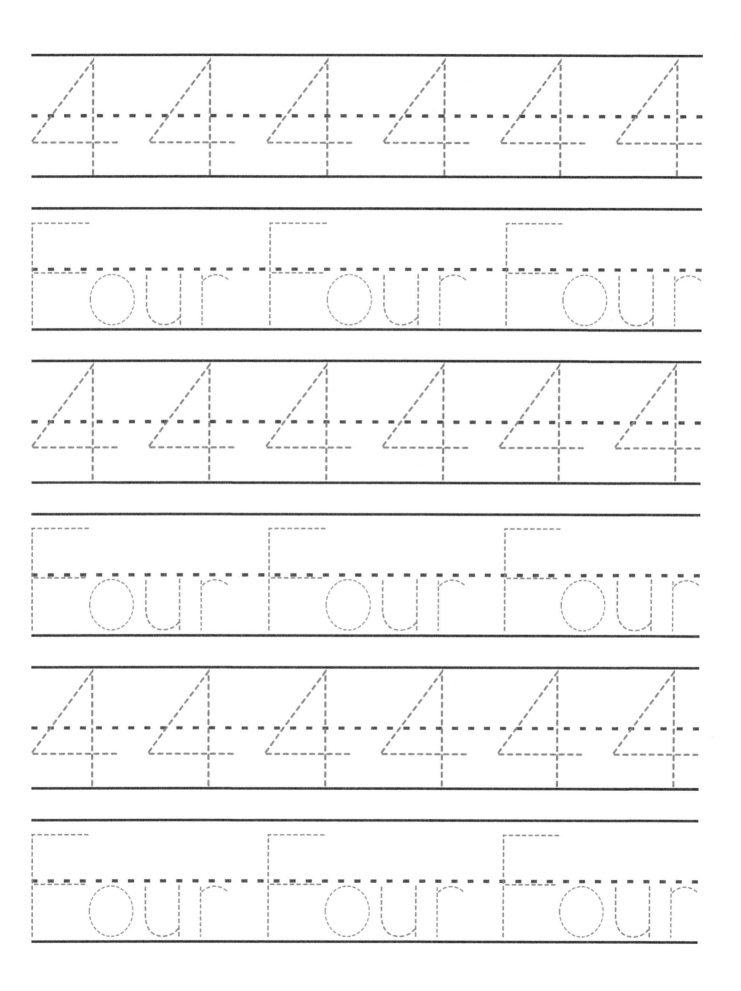

5 5 5 5 5 5

Five Five Five

5 5 5 5 5 5

Five Five Five

5 5 5 5 5 5

Five Five Five

6 Six

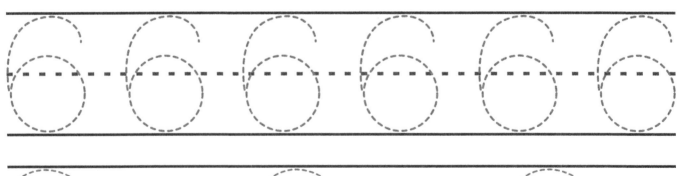

6 6 6 6 6 6

Six Six Six

6 6 6 6 6 6

Six Six Six

6 6 6 6 6 6

Six Six Six

7 Seven

7 7 7 7 7 7 7

Seven Seven

7 7 7 7 7 7 7

Seven Seven

7 7 7 7 7 7 7

Seven Seven

8 Eight

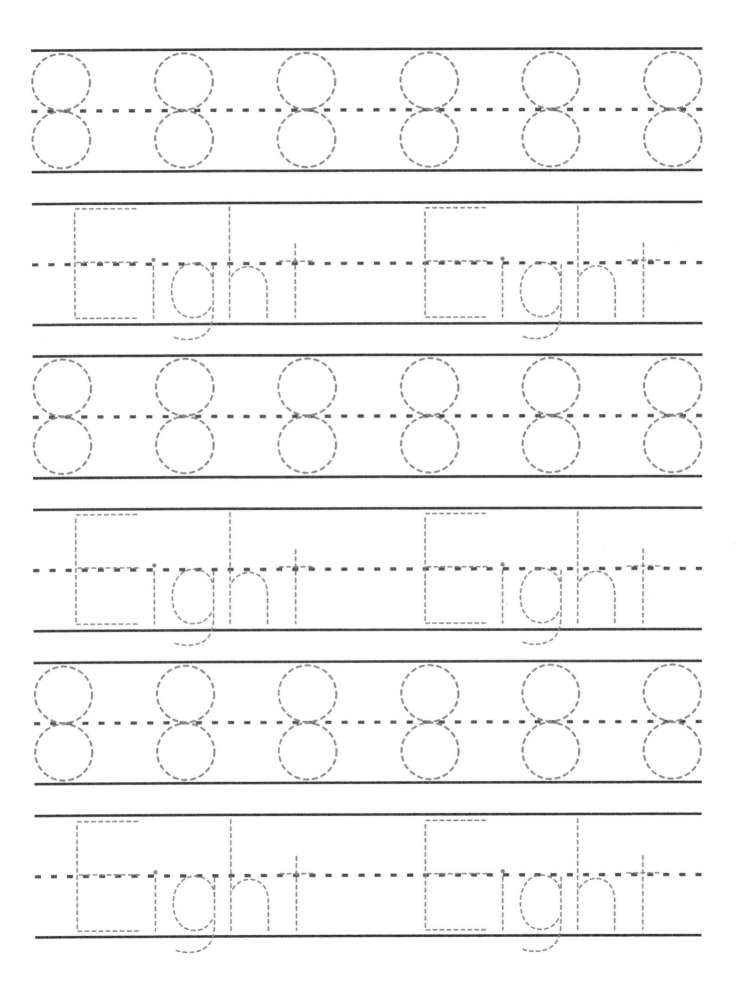

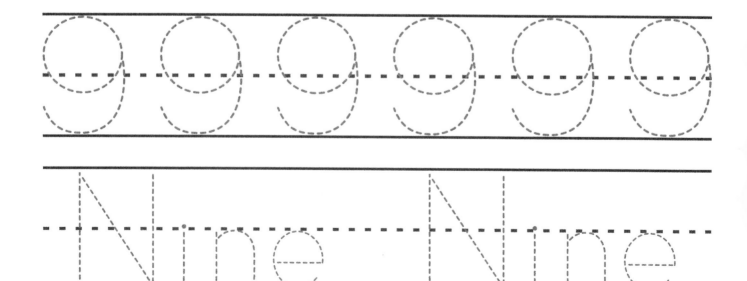

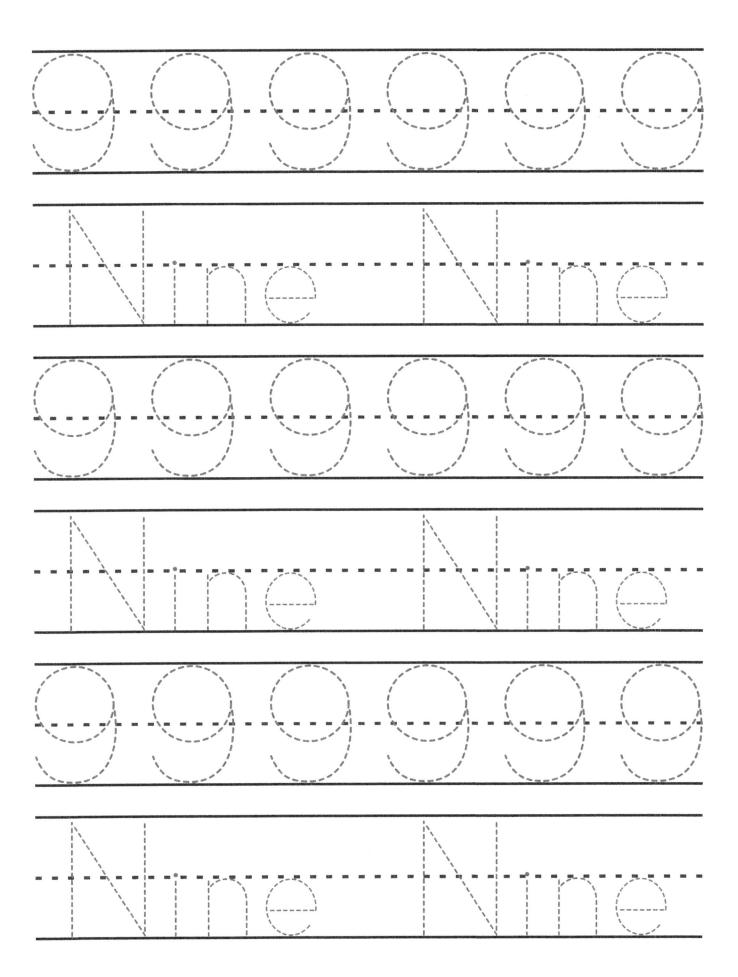

10 Ten

10 10 10

Ten Ten Ten

10 10 10

ten ten ten

10 10 10

ten ten ten

10 10 10

ten ten ten

PRACTICE ON YOUR OWN

FOLLOW US ON INSTAGRAM
@KindergartenEducation
to have a chance to win FREE notebooks

EXPLORE MORE OF OUR EDUCATIONAL NOTEBOOKS ON AMAZON

Printed in Great Britain
by Amazon